How to Better Your Worse

A Guide To Getting Your Life Together

Dedication

I want to first dedicate my first book to my Mom, Dad and my two wonderful kids. Without my Mom and Dad creating, guiding and teaching me the way of life, I don't know how far I would be in life to this day. Thank you two for laying that foundation.

Rest in Power Dad (April 23, 1948-September 27,2022)

Secondly, I want to dedicate this to my wonderful amazing Son and Daughter. They have kept me on my feet and have always made sure I was good. I am now laying the foundation down for them. I love you.

Acknowledgments

I want to acknowledge my family. My family is a field of trees with many branches and leaves. My mother was the last of 13 children. So shout out to all my aunts (esp Aunt Jo Ann) the lady that raised me as her granddaughter. To all my uncles, cousins, cousins cousins, etc.

Lastly, I want to acknowledge my 4 siblings for the being my rock and backbone when I needed it. For always being there for me through my highs and lows. They have been there to protect me and hold me accountable for anything I ever wanted to accomplish in life. They also blessed me with all my beautiful, creative and talented nieces and nephews. I could not ask for such a wonderful family.

Contents

Preface

Within this book, there are many insightful things that help us reflect on our lives. We have the control to shape it as we desire it, yet with less control over the actions of others. However, we gain power through our reactions to them. Understanding your worth brings you closer to realizing your destiny.

Once you know the REAL you, you can distinguish between what you need and what you want. Many of us often strive for what we want, overlooking what we truly need.

As you read this short but powerful guide, you will start to realize how to become your most authentic self.

Understanding your worth brings you closer to realizing your destiny.

UNIT 1

THE REAL YOU

How often do we try to figure things out on our own, only to realize we lack the information needed to do so? Frustration, anger, and doubt tend to arise, making the solution more difficult than the problem. This enhances pessimistic thoughts, creating limitations, glass ceilings, and boundaries. Sometimes, it feels like we're stuck in a never-ending cycle, running in circles but going nowhere. My father used to compare it to a dog chasing its tail, a concept I didn't fully understand until I grew older and began chasing my own tail.

When I was younger, I thought I knew it all. Nobody could tell me anything—until I realized I knew nothing at all. It wasn't until my eyes were opened that I understood my perception of life then was not what it is now. At the time, it didn't make much sense.

I remember my parents constantly telling me not to believe everything I saw or heard but to seek the truth. This instilled in me a sense of questioning. Everything I saw on television and heard on the radio was my truth. The radio taught me the latest dances and song lyrics, but I was unaware of the underlying message. On TV, I saw images of what I was supposed to look like. I still didn't understand the meaning of truth, but I knew I didn't like how it looked on me. In my process of growth, I realized my truth was different from everyone else's, which prompted me to begin seeking the Real ME.

I grew up with the best of both worlds. My mother was a stay-at-home mom, and my father worked countless hours to provide for us. I saw what it meant to have a job taking care of the necessities outside the home, while also having the responsibility of ensuring the family was taken care of inside the house. That alone taught me how life runs like a business. Whether it's working an eight-hour shift outside the house or staying home with kids for eight hours, both are full-time jobs. My parents instilled in me the belief that working hard and never giving up will get you where you want to be.

My family believed in discipline, something I know firsthand as the youngest and most inquisitive child of the four of us. I was respectful yet rebellious, sweet yet sour like a Granny Smith apple. Even though my mother kept me spiritually connected to church and in tune with the Most High, I still wanted to see what life outside of my teachings were like. I was involved in many extracurricular activities: piano, cheerleading, band, church choir, and anything else my mother could find to keep me away from the streets. It wasn't until after falling in mud holes, tripping over speed bumps, and running into roadblocks that I realized where my failures lay— the lack of knowing my worth, coupled with a misunderstanding of how life can change direction in a split second based on the choices we make. Through experiences, lessons are learned. When the struggles of life's lessons present themselves, how do you endure?

Everyone goes through transitions in life. Whether it's graduating high school, entering college, having your first child, or getting married, these are all life-changing events. But how do we handle them if we don't know how to handle them? We all think and live differently, so each outcome will be unique. However, life experiences can either make or break us, depending on how we control our actions and reactions. Facing obstacles creates lessons to be learned. The true test comes when we encounter those obstacles again, allowing us to apply what we learned during our past experiences.

Growing older opened my eyes to the fact that some of the choices I made were not becoming of me but instead consumed me. I struggled mentally, trying to figure out how to survive in this game called life. At a young age, my dreams were so big they became my destiny. I could see myself here, doing this, and that gave me joy— the joy of being somebody. When I began surrounding myself with people and environments that didn't align with my dreams, I started to adapt to that lifestyle. I not only lost sight of my dreams, but I also began to lose myself. When the mind loses control, negative influences easily take hold of the soul. I became a person outside of my own body, looking at my lowest self. Seeing my weak flesh left me meek and distraught.

The light bulb finally went off when I realized that the people I surrounded myself with influenced my bad habits and poor decisions. Detaching from toxic energy and re-planning my future by setting goals helped me start picking up the pieces of myself. This transition allowed me to create life goals based on what I wanted to accomplish and what to avoid. I broke it down by how long it would take and what it would require to get there. Achieving my goals didn't come without obstacles, transitions, and setbacks, but these challenges shaped me into who I am today. After finally understanding my destiny, I now wake up glowing every day, knowing that my faith and perseverance helped me discover God's purpose for me.

When you're at your lowest, how do you pick yourself back up? Do you pretend like you have a grip on life, or do you reflect on the lessons you've learned and apply them to your future decisions?

I share these stories because no one's life is perfect. We've all experienced low moments. The only reason I was able to pick myself back up was because I made the decision to Better My Worst enemy—myself. This book is both inspirational and self-motivational. It provides insights on how to navigate your present life while preparing for your future destiny. No one can live your life better than you can. Whether you're young or old, your future depends on you.

Below is a blank section for you to reflect on a time when you discovered your truth. How did that change your perspective on life? What lesson did you learn from the experience that could help someone else?

_____

_____

_____

_____

_____

_____

_____

_____

_____

_____

People may try to give you all the advice in the world, but until they've walked in your shoes, they will never truly know your journey. The more we grow and evolve, the more we become aware of who and what we are. Everyone has a purpose for living, breathing, and blooming. What is your purpose? The answer lies in how much you trust your faith.

"How can you be you, if you don't know what you really look like?"-Cree

UNIT 2

SETTING LIFE GOALS

What are goals? What purpose do they serve in life? Why are goals necessary if they take so long to achieve?

When thinking about setting goals for your life, what's the first thing that comes to mind? It might be things you desire, money you need, or even where you see yourself in the future. How does someone take steps to make these things happen? Where do you start? Will patience be something you learn, or will it get in the way? Many obstacles and challenges will come up, but in the end, it's all about navigating your road map toward your destiny.

I didn't fully understand the meaning of goals until I created and followed some myself. For me, goals connect to sports. For example, in basketball, the ball is shot into the basket; in football, the ball is kicked between two poles; and in hockey, the puck has to pass the goalie to reach the net. These are all examples of goals where the object of each sport represents reaching its destination.

Life is like the sports we love and watch so faithfully. We sometimes forget the important things in life because we get so caught up in celebrating others' victories. Sunday night football would come on, and my mom would be cooking while watching her favorite team. She'd be so focused on them winning that sometimes the water from the potatoes would start boiling over, sizzling on the stove and momentarily distracting her. Still, she kept her eyes on that touchdown while knowing her goal was to feed us.

Many of us see life as a game, but I see it as a business. Challenges arise, life gets harder, and distractions can take our focus off of faith. Life's not easy when there's so much pulling us in different directions. The biggest obstacle in going after what you want is staying focused. Imagine it's the night of the season finale of your favorite show, but finals are in the morning. Which would take priority?

Setting priorities, from most important to least, gives you direction. Taking it one step at a time will get you to the top. Create a system with realistic timelines to achieve realistic goals. Once you've got a deadline, the key is not to miss it. At the beginning of each semester, we're given a syllabus with due dates for assignments. In my senior year, I waited until the night before to finish something I could've done weeks earlier. Staying up all night to get it done was stressful. I did well, but cramming at the last minute wasn't worth it. Although I met the deadline, I learned from it.

Goal-setting works the same way. To stay grounded while meeting deadlines, set specific dates. Whether it takes days, months, or years to accomplish, make it happen.

At around 8 or 9 years old, I already had a vision of where and what I wanted to be. I knew college and grad school would be part of the journey, along with owning a house by a certain age and being an entrepreneur. As the years went by, I realized that reaching my goals depended on following *my* road map to success. Notice I emphasize "MY" because only you can plan, prepare, and execute your destiny. So, gather the right resources and gear up for the journey. Don't waste the time that belongs to you.

Here's a model to help set and organize your goals. This approach starts with five goals, from urgent to desirable, short-term to long-term. Beginning with just five goals is a good way to get your mind focused on *you* and what you want out of life. Stay focused on what's current and build from there. Each goal will include the how, where, when, and why. This keeps each task relevant, moving you closer to your destination.

Start: Short-term to Long-term	Goals	How long will it take to accomplish?	Where is the starting point?	When will time be made to implement the plan?	Why do I want to pursue this goal?
Goal 1					
Goal 2					
Goal 3					
Goal 4					
Goal 5					

After reviewing the model, you might think, *Now what?* Don't panic. Think about each goal, from least to most important, short-term to long-term. Organize them based on what you want to achieve first, with realistic intentions. As you work toward the later goals, they may take longer and require more effort.

Here are some tips to help map out your road to success:

How long will it take to accomplish?

- How much time do I need to put in daily?
- Will this take weeks, months, or years?

10

- How dedicated am I to completing it?

Where is the starting point?

- What resources are needed?

- Do I already have access to what I need?

- What research could help my plan?

When will I make time to work on the plan?

- When can I focus on my goals and put other activities aside?

- Is this something I can work on short-term or long-term?

- When will I begin doing the work?

Why do I want to pursue this goal?

- Has this always been a passion?

- Why am I so interested in this goal?

- How can I improve myself by achieving this?

After filling in the table, make it big enough to see every day—on a poster board, vision board, or chalkboard. Go big so you'll always see it.

"When you do positive things consistently, you build the energy to create positive outcomes!"-Cree

UNIT 3

THE BALANCING ACT

At this point in the book, everything we've discussed should be ready for you to put into action. First, we talked about understanding and truly knowing the real you. Then, after getting to know who you are and where you're headed, we covered how to put that plan in motion. Remember, where we come from never determines where we're trying to go, no matter the phase, stage, or age you're at in life. Believing in each goal reflects who you are and defines your purpose in life.

As you move toward each destination, obstacles are bound to pop up. How do you deal with those challenges when they do? Do you stop, give up without considering the finish line? Or do you push forward, get over the bumps, and claim the reward at the end?

When it comes to having a regular, paying job, sometimes it just is what it is. Maybe there's no ladder to climb, no vision of where you'll be in the company in ten years. Once you've reached the highest level there, boredom kicks in, along with that restless feeling of "what's next?" I remember in one of my many jobs, around six months in, the work became boring. It started out great because it was new, but after I mastered everything, I was ready to move on to something bigger and better. I felt eager but frustrated, which led me to resent the job I once loved. But since I had to provide for my family, I had to balance things out and ask myself, "What's next?" When I finally moved to another job, I could apply what I'd learned to help me land other positions. That felt good because it meant I made more money.

Using the balancing act system means leveraging your life between where you are now and where you want to be in the future. I keep stressing this because a lot of people think it's too late. But it's never too late to fulfill your destiny, even if it's on a smaller scale—you've still reached your goals. By setting realistic goals and motivating yourself to complete them, you're already on the road to your destiny.

Now the picture of where you could be is clearer. Your visions and dreams have been mapped out to become realities. Whether it's leaving the 9-to-5 grind and starting your own business, the struggle is real, but the reward is worth it. We all have reasons why we want to improve ourselves. It can be hard to break out of the norm if you don't know how. So, how can it be done?

In tough situations, we often let our emotions make decisions for us instead of using common sense. Sometimes, sticking it out and figuring things out relieves the stress of going without. I know that might not make sense now, but it will when the time is right.

As you map out your career, use each job as a chance to learn something you can apply down the road. You've got to keep a "WHAT'S NEXT" mentality—not only to finish a goal but to be ready to create new ones.

The table in the previous chapter serves as a platform to build a purpose timeline, positioning each goal based on how long it will take to achieve it. Meanwhile, life doesn't stop.

"Achieving a mission takes hard work and dedication. It all depends on how hard YOU go to accomplish it." -Cree

UNIT 4

THE BREAKTHROUGH

What is a breakthrough? What does it mean when applied to life? Here's what a Breakthrough looks like to me:

- Being
- Realistic
- Evolving
- Apprehension
- Knowing
- Trust
- Humbleness
- Reflecting
- Outcomes
- Unleash
- Goals
- Hesitation

Being Realistic in **Evolving** with the **Apprehension** of **Knowing** that we must **Trust** through **Humbleness**, **Reflecting** on **Outcomes** that **Unleash** new **Goals** without **Hesitation**. This may sound abstract, but breaking it down, each letter represents what it takes to become great. Not only do we want to reach the next level, but we want to be great at getting there. To make this clearer, here's the breakdown:

Being who you are is crucial before moving forward in life. Sometimes, we're around people who make us feel out of place, maybe because we don't know how to fit in. It's essential to know what you like and dislike. This helps you understand who you can tolerate and how to handle others. In life, on this journey, many languages are spoken—not always foreign. If we don't allow ourselves to connect with the world around us, we'll keep running into roadblocks.

When you know yourself, your choices reflect who you are. You start doing things based on what *you* like, not just what others do. There's an unbelievable feeling of control over your destiny when you make choices true to yourself.

Realistic thoughts bring realistic outcomes. What's achieved comes from what's believed. This acronym shows you can reach, maintain, and sustain anything in life if it's real. Don't sell yourself short, but make sure your goals are based on something actual and factual—not some fantasy you know deep down won't be completed. Think about what makes your goal a reality, not just a dream. If fantasy keeps calling, reconsider your path. Be real with yourself by knowing who you are and your worth.

Evolving into who you are brings clarity. Once that lightbulb goes off, you start seeing things that were hidden before. The picture in plain sight all along suddenly becomes clear. Many of us adapt to our surroundings; that's why it's important *not* to be a product of your environment. Growing up, I thought I knew a lot, but looking back, I knew nothing. Becoming an adult brought change—my thoughts, my walk, and my talk evolved with me. That's how we evolve as people. It's up to us to seek growth, to keep evolving.

Apprehension can create tension in the vision. Anxiety can be your best friend or worst enemy. It can take you places you never imagined. Apprehension draws the line between what we should or shouldn't do based on our feelings. When we let emotions overrule common sense, we're more likely to fail. Listen to that inner voice—the one saying "go right" when you're about to go left. When making decisions, follow the positive energy in you. Don't lose sight of the purpose.

Knowing your worth is one of life's biggest challenges. Not knowing who you are can lead to paths of destruction, trapping you in cycles. Getting caught up in what others are doing takes focus away from your journey. Learning how the world works with *you* in it means more than just liking or disliking things; it's about handling adversity, showing leadership for those who look up to you, and diffusing situations without reacting emotionally. Know your place in the world by showing up with faith and action.

Trust in yourself. Again, know your worth and who you are. No one can take that from you. When your foundation is solid, it's hard for anything to interfere. The only damage is what *you* allow. If you don't trust yourself, how can you expect others to trust you? Be confident that everything will fall into place. Trust has to be a priority to keep you steady on your path.

Humbleness pays off. Staying humble in what you do relaxes the mind, body, and soul. If you're an overthinker or lack patience, practice humility. Don't jump the gun when things don't happen as quickly as expected. We're quick to give up if we feel defeated, but challenges shape the outcome. If one piece of the puzzle doesn't fit, put it aside, rethink, and try a new piece.

Respect the process. As you go through the motions, be mindful of who you let in your circle. Sometimes, when we confide in certain people, their words can dampen our fire. The passion that was once there fades. Don't let anyone dictate your path—that's disrespecting the journey. There will always be people saying what can't be done. Surrounding yourself with negativity won't bring positive results. If you know in your heart it's right, respect yourself enough to push through. And anyone not willing to ride with you? Roll right past them.

Outcomes depend on how you progress. Think about it like getting your hair done—you sit in that chair, waiting to see the final look. Life's outcomes are built on the time and persistence you invest.

Unleash the inner beast. Everyone has a little Lion in them. Don't hold back when that animal inside you requires to be tapped into.

Goals, goals, goals! Setting and achieving goals can't be emphasized enough. The more willpower you gather to reach one goal, the more likely you'll set and achieve more. It's a cycle of growth. If the sky is your limit, what does your sky look like?

Hesitation kills motivation. When opportunities arise, we're sometimes overwhelmed, and we hesitate. Even with positive energy, there's that little doubt whispering, "Should I?" Overthinking can kill the vibe. It's okay to think things through, but ultimately, the decision is between you and your purpose. Don't hold back the gifts you have—you might regret it later.

When barriers are broken, growth is unstoppable. Waking up every day full of joy is something we all need and deserve. Stop letting the weight of the world dictate your path. Never be someone you're not. Never let anyone take your identity. Never give up.

"When the foundation is solid, it can only be damaged because you allowed it. The BREAKTHROUGH is on YOU!" -Cree

UNIT 5

KEEPING IT MOVING

On the path to destiny, mistakes will be made. Shortcomings will show up, along with roadblocks that just can't be moved. It's up to us to know that no matter what, nothing will stop what we deserve.

But why do we spend so much time stuck in the past? Getting consumed by what she said or what he did, letting the thick smoke blind us from seeing past today. Why is that? Why waste positive energy on negative people?

Just the other morning, I was taking my daughter to school. Now, let me tell you—I'm not a morning person, so mornings are always a little rough for me. But on this particular day, my spirits were up. It was a Friday, and knowing the weekend was just around the corner had me feeling good.

After I dropped her off and was getting on the highway, my good mood even allowed me let someone cut in front of me. With good intentions. But apparently, the lady behind me wasn't having it. She started blowing her horn, almost ramming into the back of my car. By this time, my reaction matched her energy—I blew my horn back and stared her down in the rearview mirror. For about four seconds, we held up traffic, both of us looking ridiculous. When I finally pulled off, I was livid.

But as I calmed down, I asked myself, "Why are you letting her mess with your happiness?" Moments like these show how easily we get rattled by other people's ignorance.

Or what about when you and your boyfriend call it quits? It might take a few days—or weeks—to get over him, but time heals

21

all wounds. After a few months, you're back to being you. You're trying new things, stepping out of your comfort zone, and discovering yourself. Then one day, you're out at the mall with your friends, having the best time ever, and BAM—you see him. The guy who broke your heart so bad you couldn't eat for a week.

Seeing him messes with your vibe. Now, you're spending days replaying everything in your head. But here's the real question: Would you let him drag you back into that dark place? Or would you laugh it off because your life without him is a thousand times better?

These are the reasons why knowing how to keep it moving is crucial. I used to tell my kids when they'd get upset and cry, "Are you crying because you're that mad, or because you don't know what to do with your feelings?" Nine times out of ten, they'd stop crying right there, thinking about my words.

I remember when my son first started liking girls. There was this one time he was really upset with one of them. Of course, as his mom, I was ready to roll up and talk to her mom, like, "What's up with your daughter upsetting my son?" But after talking to him, I realized he wasn't mad about something she did—he was upset for her. She was going through her own struggles, and he cared so much that he let it affect him.

Obstacles, challenges, fears—they'll always pop up when you're on your grind. And no, GRIND isn't just about making money. It stands for Get Real Involved Not Distraught. Grinding means getting your life together, not just chasing a check.

Whatever's blocking your path—whether you roll over it, stop to move it, or realize you're on the wrong road—it's all part of the process.

"Adapt to the changes, don't let anything or anyone dictate your journey, and keep it moving. Your goals will become your reality."
-Cree

REFLECTIONS

This book is full of insights that allows us to reflect on life. We have control over how we shape our lives, but not over other people's actions. What we can control is how we react. When you know your worth, you're one step closer to realizing your destiny.

Once you figure out the real you, you'll see the difference between what you need and what you want. Too often, we chase wants and ignore our needs. It's like wanting a Mercedes when you've got Ford money. You can afford the Ford, and it gets the job done, but chasing that Mercedes will only put you in debt.

Don't be scared to conquer your goals. Go for it, the time is always yours to use and start a new. Continue to want and dream for the things you know to be factual and make those dreams your reality. Move in your light and your purpose. You only have yourself, so make your worst your best while your still willing and able.

"As life threw curveballs at me, I still pushed through with faith. Walking in my light, towards my purpose makes life much greater." – Cree